Just Like Me Series

Copyright © 2010 Just Like Me, Inc.

AF270829

Ancient African Discoveries
Take a trip into ancient history to
discover the contributions of
ancient African scientists

African American Inventions
Discover African American
inventions that changed our society

Future Careers
Journey into the future to see what
you will be when you grow-up

Just Like Me, Inc.
Washington, DC 20017
(202) 526-1725

First Edition - First Printing
September 2010

ISBN 978-1928889045

Table of Contents

Book 1 of the Just Like Me Series (Ancient African Discoveries) 4

- Discoveries ranging from mathematics to the 365 day calendar

- Activity Pages that reinforce the lessons learned in the book

- Source materials used in creating this book

Book 2 of the Just Like Me Series (African American Inventions) 41

- Inventions that Changed Society

- Activity Pages that reinforce the lessons learned in the book

- Approved Patents from the U.S. Patent Office

Book 3 of the Just Like Me Series (Careers) 84

- Hobbies that can be turned into rewarding careers

- Activity Pages that reinforce the lessons learned in the book

- A Message of success

The Just Like Me Series is a combination of three separate successful books combined into one amazing series. Each book is separated by its original title page.

Just Like Me

THE BEGINNING OF CIVILIZATION

Text by
Yaba Baker

Illustrations by
Anne Marie Oldham

Just Like Me, Inc.
Washington, DC 20017
(202) 526-1725

Fifth Edition - Fifth Printing
September 2010

African scientists were the first to create mathematics like addition, subtraction, multiplication, division, and fractions. African scientists went on to create higher level mathematics like geometry and trigonometry. These early discoveries made it possible to later create things like computers, microwaves, and televisions that we use today.

African people were the first to create a school of higher learning, which is now called a college or a university.

Afican Scientist created the divisions of time (seconds, minutes, hours, and days).

6:00 A.M.

Each weekday has 12 hours of the day and 12 hours of the night, which was discovered by African scientists. The scientists discovered that it takes exactly 24 hours for earth to have day and night.

6:00

Each weekday has 24 hours in it. When the 24 hours is up, the weekday changes. Monday has 24 hours and when Monday's 24 hours are up, Tuesday's 24 hours begins.

6:00 A.M.

African people were the first people to farm and use animals to help with farming.

Africans in several different areas of Africa were the first people to invent tools such as hand axes, arrows, and fish hooks which were necessary to build communities.

African people were the first people to build a community into a city with craft workers, soldiers, and priests. The farmers in the surrounding countryside provided food for the city workers by raising wheat, barley, cattle, and goats.

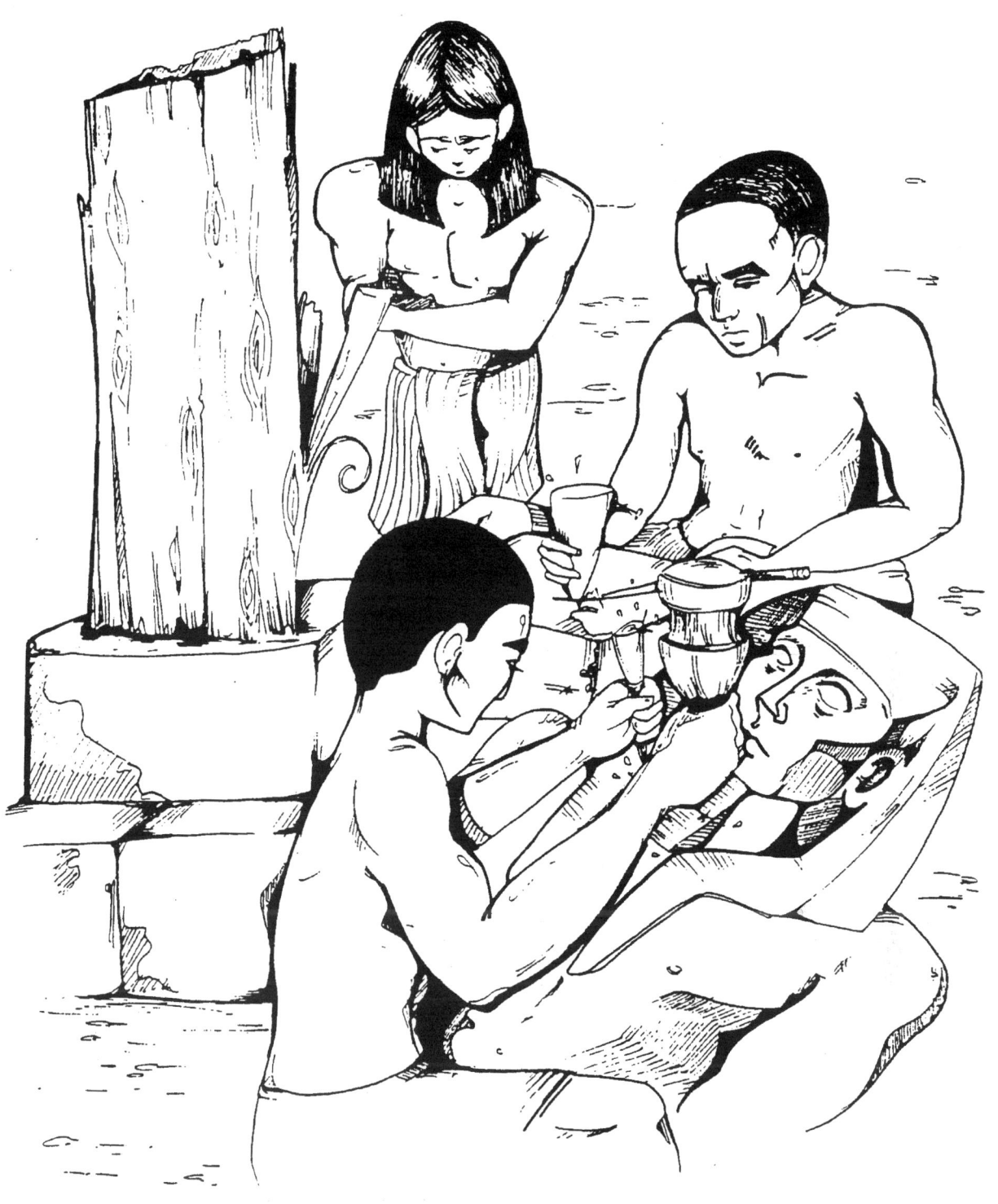

Africans were excellent in creating different forms of art. Statues were made of many different materials from wood to the hardest stone called black diorite.

The first people on earth were Africans.

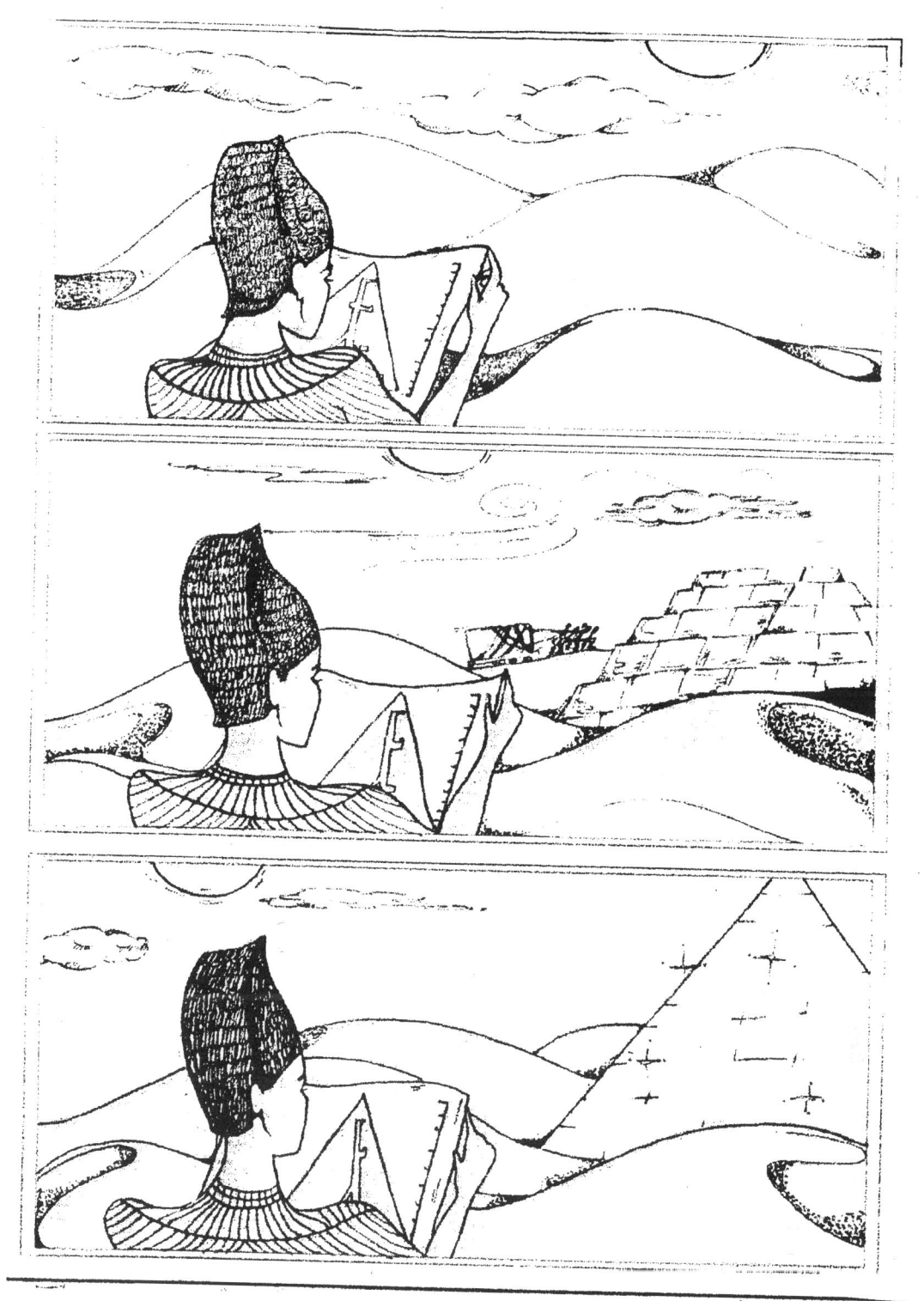

An African scientist and architect named Imhotep built the first pyramid as a place to study the stars, as well as a place to bury dead pharaohs (kings). This pyramid is the oldest standing stone monument in the world, still standing some 4,600 years later.

North America

South America

All men and women came from Africa. As time went on, men and women moved to different parts of the world. The differences in temperature in these various parts of the world caused changes in the features of the nose,

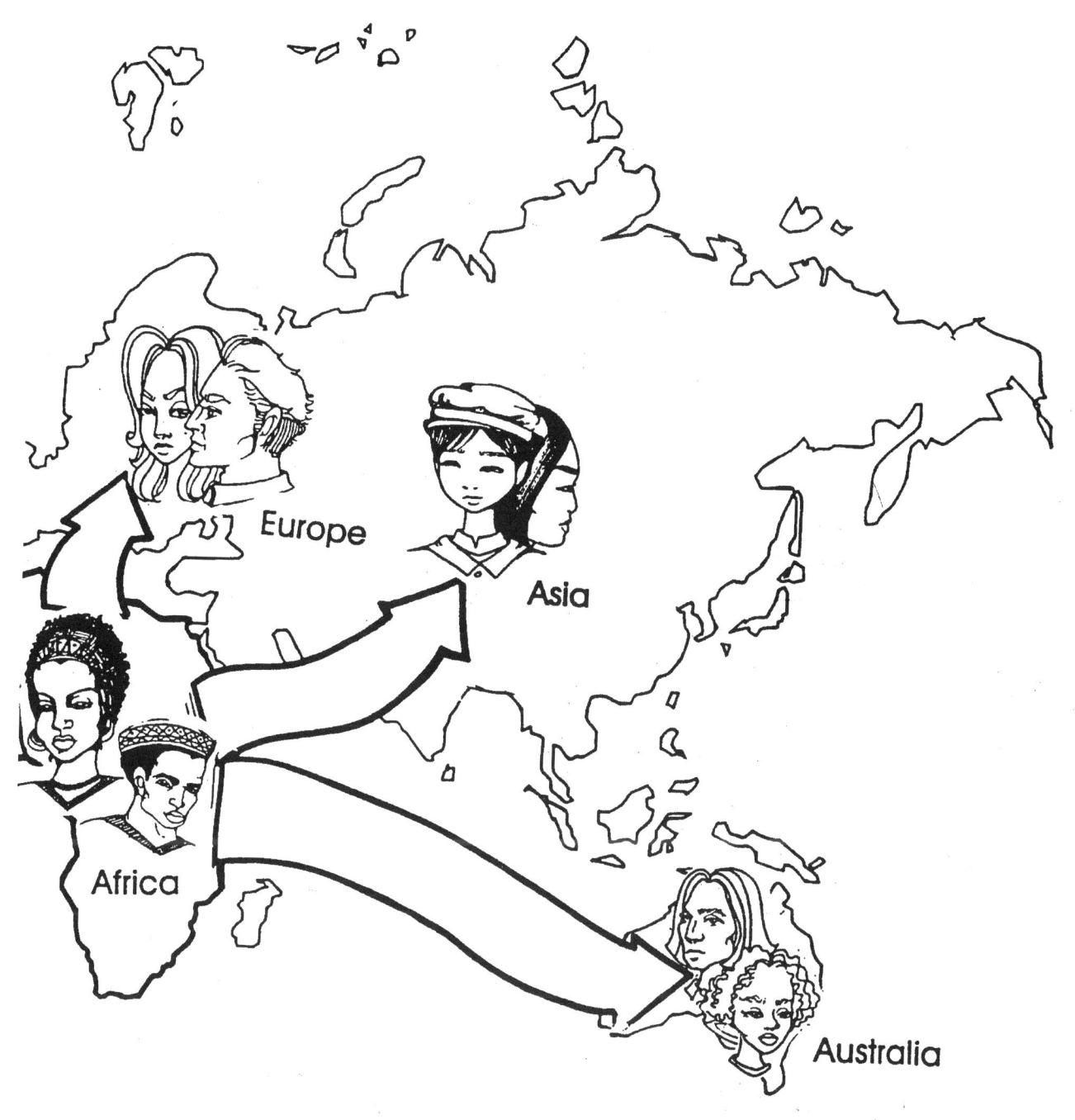

hair, skin color and eye color to adapt to the temperature. This is why there are different races such as Africans, Caucasians, Asians, Native Americans, Latinos and so on.

African architects built the pyramids so precisely, the four corners face exactly to the north pole, south pole, east, and west.

Egypt

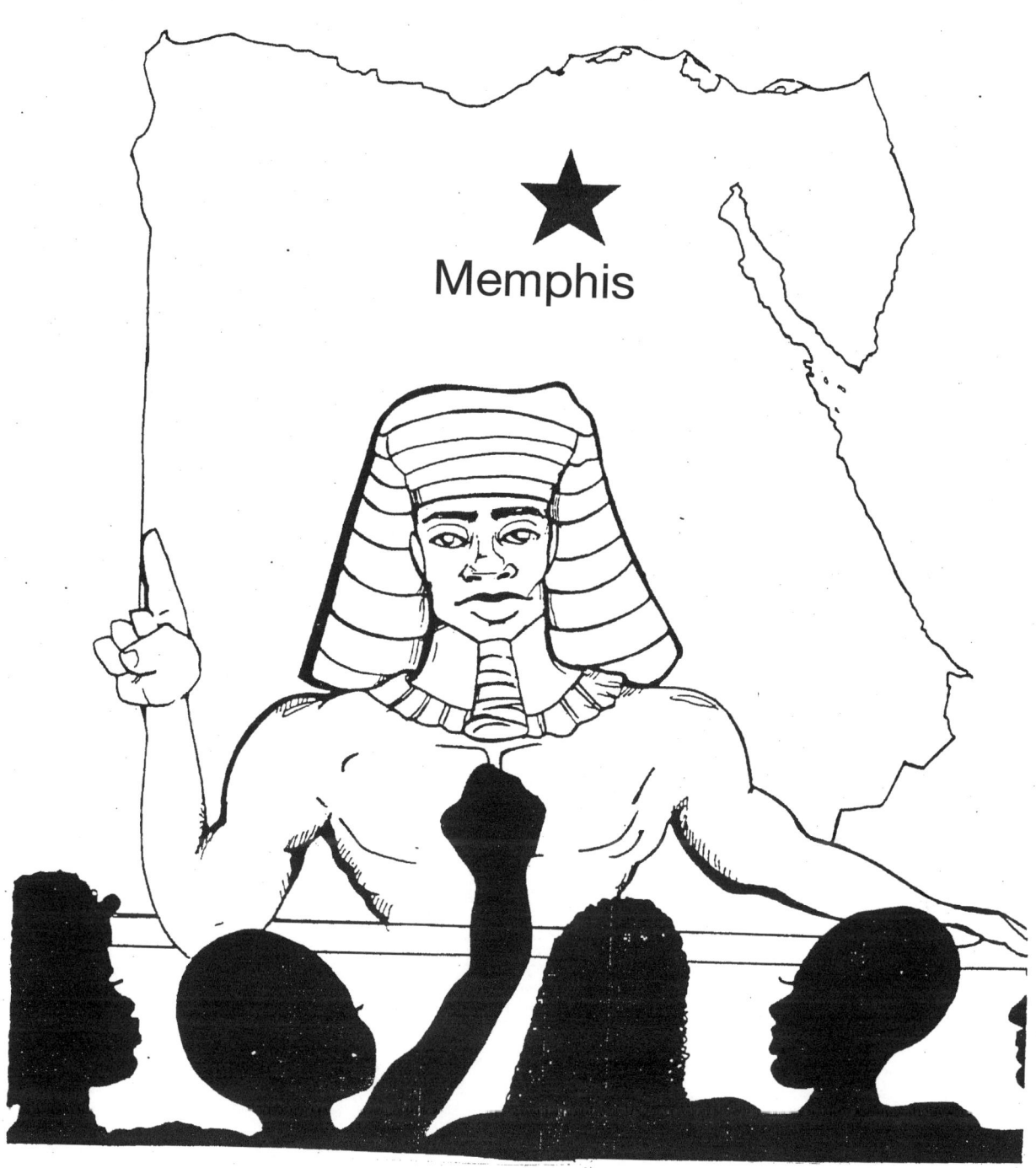

Memphis

African people formed two territories, which were called the lands of Upper Egypt and Lower Egypt. Later, Upper and Lower Egypt became the world's first unified country. Menes was the king who unified Egypt and created the first known government in the world. Egypt was ruled by a Pharaoh (king).

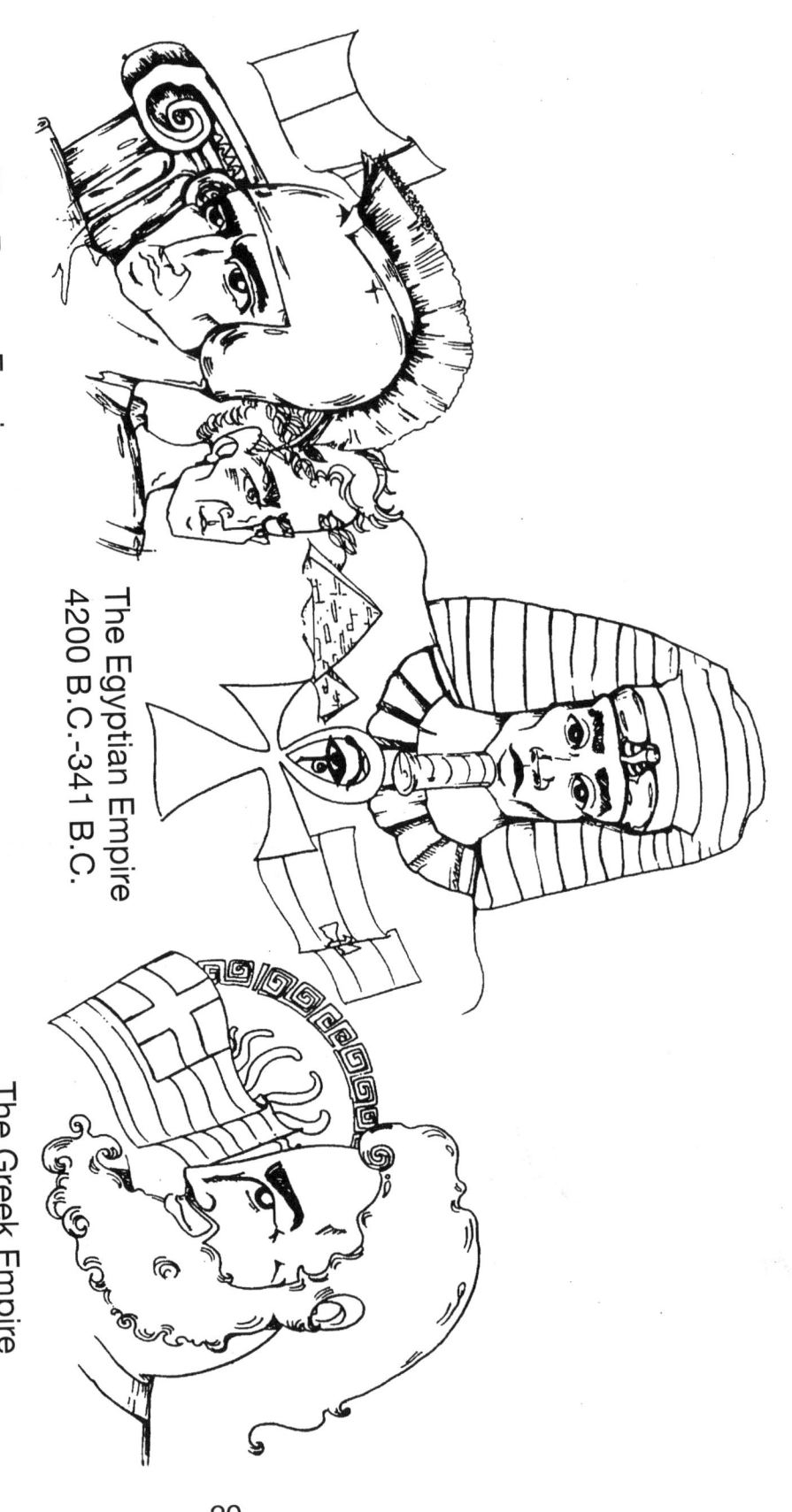

The Roman Empire
202 B.C.-476 A.D.

The Egyptian Empire
4200 B.C.-341 B.C.

The Greek Empire
1100 B.C.-323 B.C.

The Egyptian civilization lasted over 3000 years. Roman and Greek empires combined, only lasted about 1400 years. The United States is only 234 years old. Therefore, the African civilization is one of the oldest known civilizations in the world.

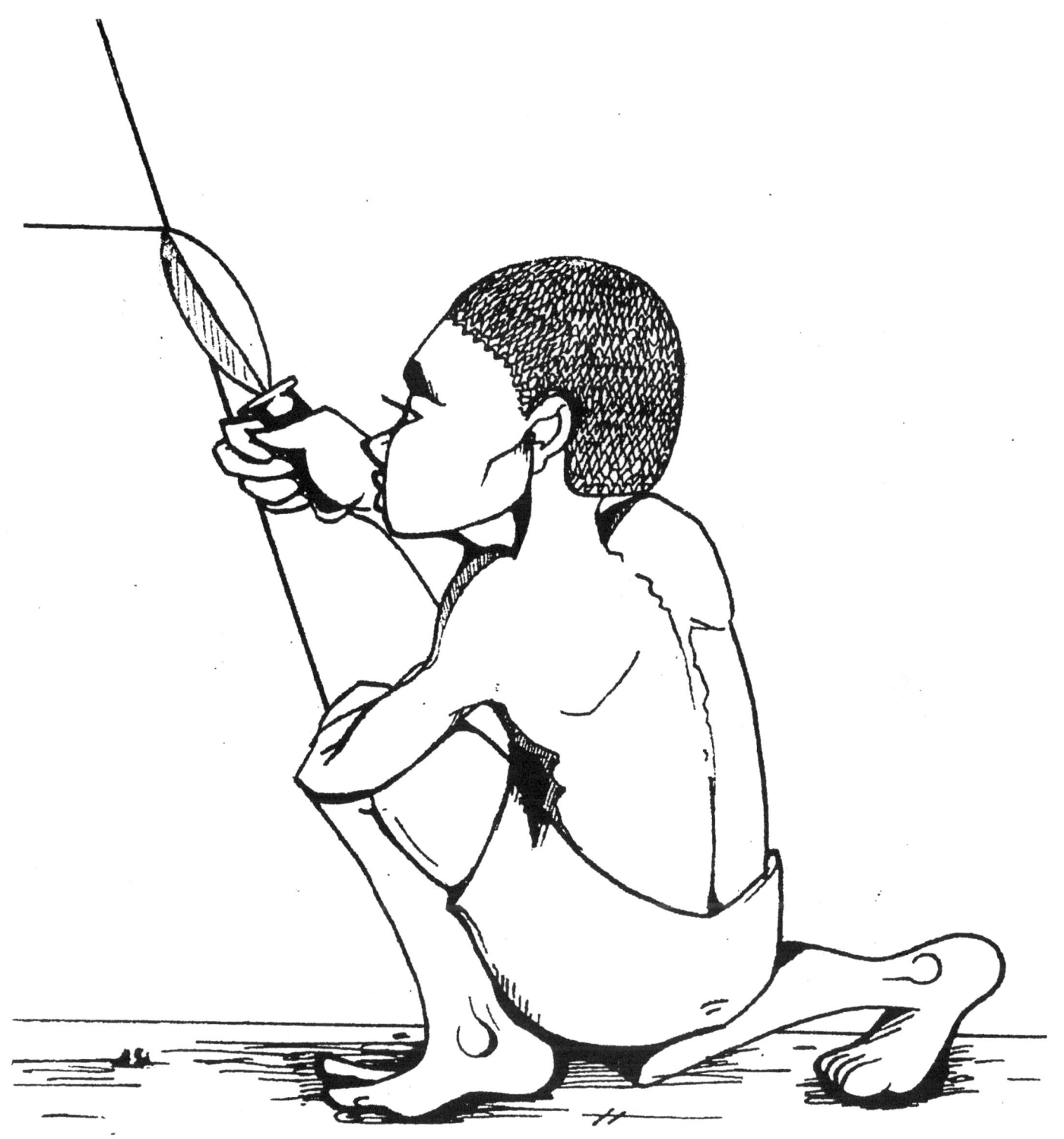

The pyramids were built without using concrete or any type of glue to hold the pyramids together. Instead, the pyramids were built by placing blocks of stone on top of each other. The African craftsmen cut the blocks so perfectly and the blocks fit so tightly on top of each other, that a knife could not fit between the blocks.

Pyramids were built using blocks that weighed from 2 tons to 70 tons. The smallest block used in building the pyramids equaled the weight of 2 cars.

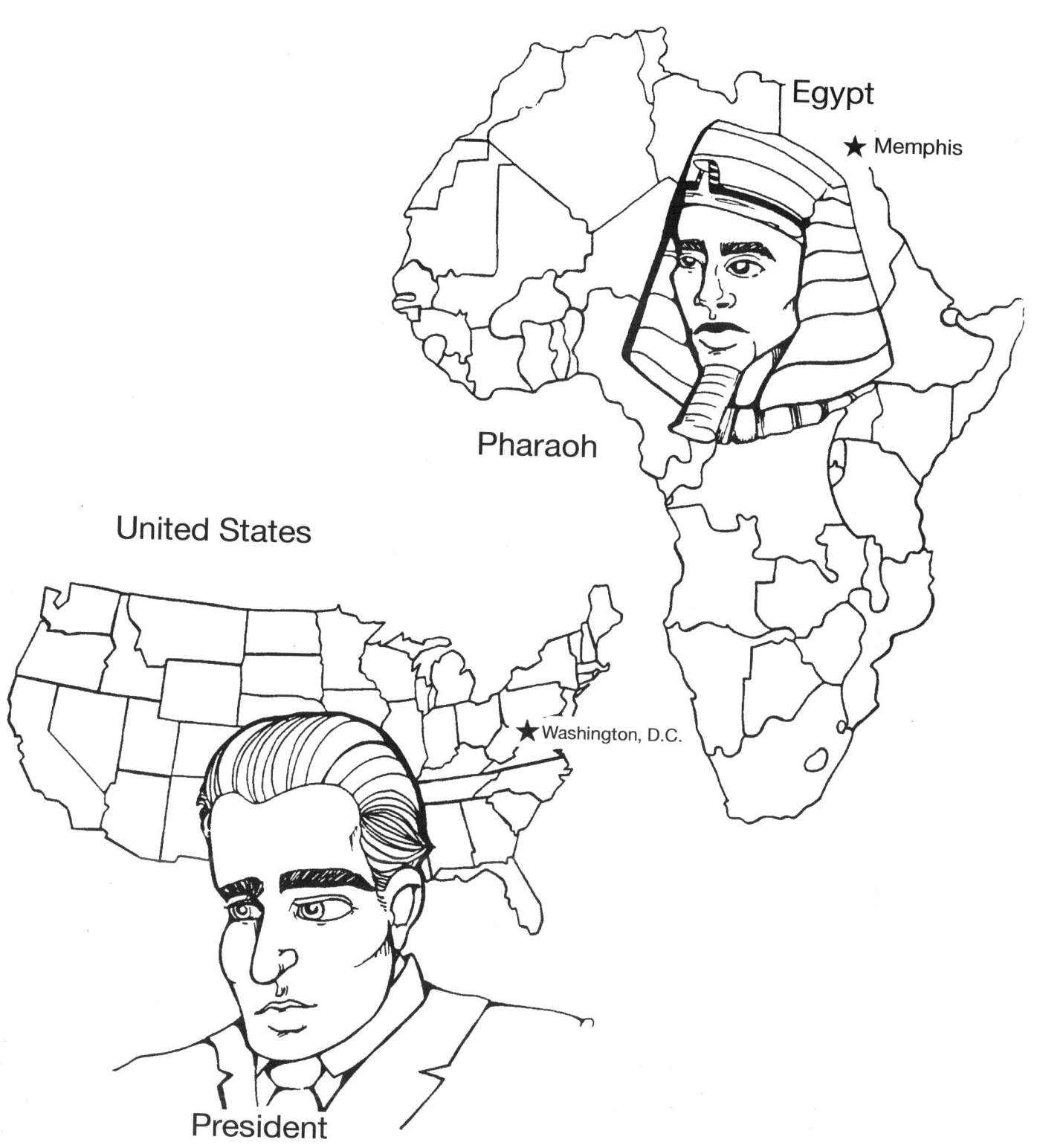

Egypt

★ Memphis

Pharaoh

United States

★ Washington, D.C.

President

Menes created a city called Memphis to serve as the capital city for Egypt. Memphis was the capital of Egypt like Washington, D.C. is the capital of the United States.

Africans were experts at the craft of pottery as well as painting. Even today, African pottery is considered works of genius.

Obelisk

(an ancient African monument)

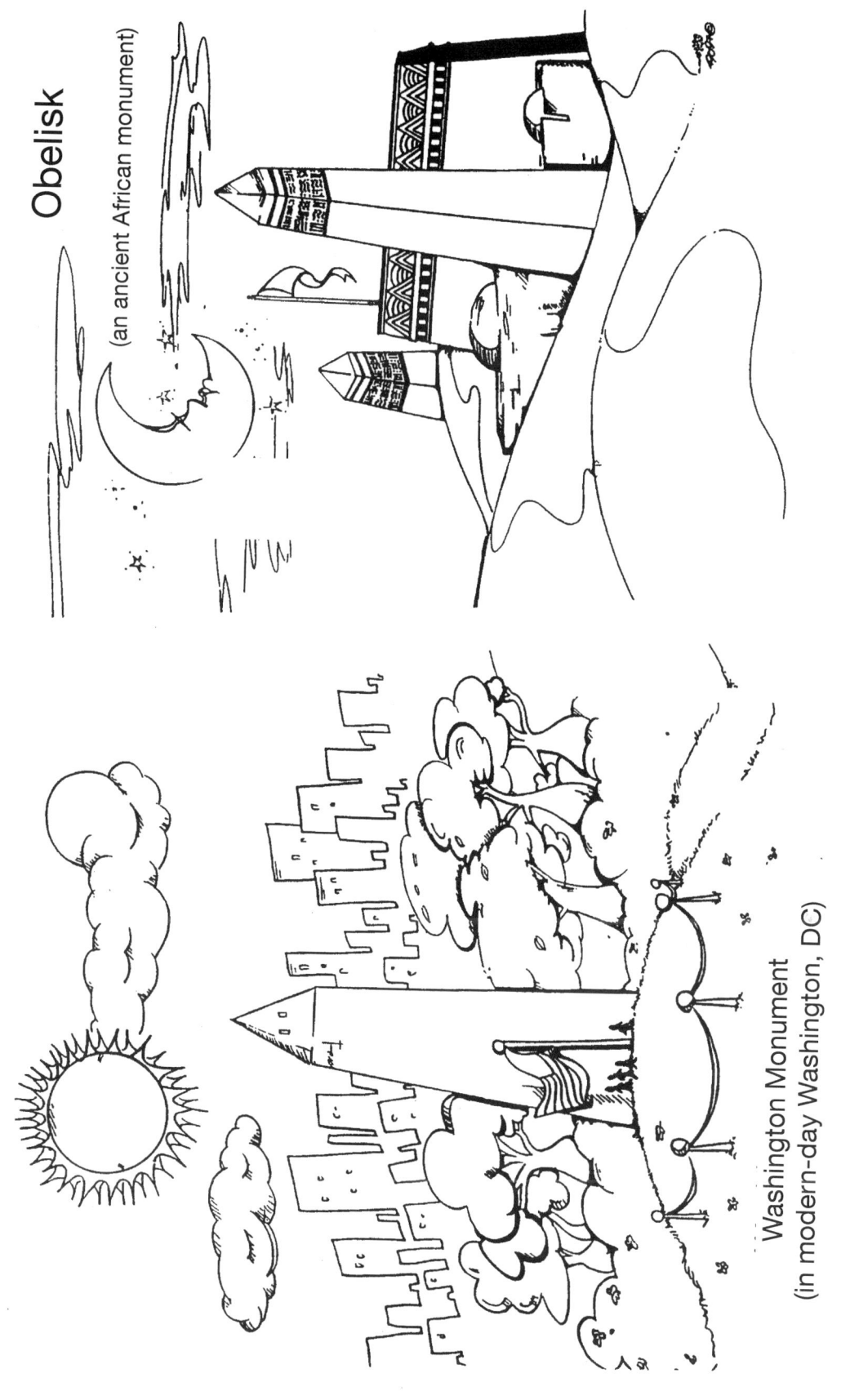

Washington Monument
(in modern-day Washington, DC)

African architecture was so advanced that it was the basis for some modern architecture. In fact, the Washington Monument is an exact duplicate of an African monument originally called a Tekhen (renamed later as an Obelisk).

Africans in Egypt created the first kind of paper and ink to write with that was small and light to carry.

African doctors had become skilled in examination, diagnosis, and treatment of over 250 illnesses. Records showed treatments of different injuries which included numerous surgical techniques.

African scientist discovered the 365 day calendar year. These scientists were the first to discover that there are 365 days in a year that can be divided into 12 months.

African people created civilization. Without African scientists, doctors, astronomers, mathematicians, and leaders, our society as we know it, would not exist. *Africans and African Americans are intelligent, beautiful people with a rich history. Everyone should know how each race has contributed to the world we know today. Take what you have learned today and share it with someone you know.*

Draw and color how life would be without ink and paper.

Africans created math. Draw and color a picture of how life would be without math.

Africans were the first to build communities. Draw and color a picture of your community (neighborhood).

Draw and color a picture of the Washington Monument
and the African Monument called the Tekhen.

What tools helped build the African community? Draw
and color those tools.

The first doctors were in Africa. Draw and color a trip to the doctor.

Africans built the pyramids. Draw and color a pyramid.

African scientist discovered that it takes 24 hours to have day and night. Draw and color what you do in the day and what you do at night.

Africans were the first people to farm. Draw and color some animals you might find on a farm today.

Where is Africa? Draw and color the continent of Africa.

THE BEGINNING OF CIVILIZATION
BIBLIOGRAPHY

Diop, Cheikh, <u>The African Origin of Civilization Myth or Reality</u>, Chicago, Illinois, Lawrence Hill Books, 1974.

James, George, <u>Stolen Legacy</u>, Trenton, NJ, African World Press, 1954.

Tarharka, Keita, <u>Black Manhood</u>, Washington, D.C., University Press of America, 1979.

"The Grandeur That Was Nubia," <u>The Washington Post</u>, May 10, 1995, p. H1.

"Early African Bone Tools Found," <u>The Washington Post</u>, April 28, 1995, p. A1.

Murray, Margaret, <u>The Splendor That Was Egypt</u>, New York, Philosophical Library, 1957.

Just Like Me

How African-American Inventions Changed America

Copyright © 1996 Just Like Me, Inc.

Text by
Yaba Baker

Edited by
Jarda Alexander

Illustrations by
Leslie Quill

Just Like Me, Inc.
Washington, DC 20017
(202) 526-1725

Seventh Edition-Seventh Printing
September 2010

George F. Grant developed the **golf tee** in 1899, which is a small wooden peg used to hold a golf ball in place. Grant invented the golf tee because he and other golfers had trouble keeping the ball still on the initial drive.

J. Stanard made the first truly workable **refrigerator** in 1891. Other refrigerators did not cool properly and food often spoiled. Stanard's brilliant use of compressed air and the correct amount of ether as a coolant is what made his refrigerator such a success.

One of the first **ironing boards** was created by **Sarah Boone** in 1892.
It was a long narrow wooden board with padded-cloth and folding legs.
Before the creation of the ironing board, people ironed on tables.

An early version of the **clothes dryer** was invented by **George T. Sampson** in 1892. It was one of the first machines to use a motor to dry clothing. Before the clothes dryer, clothes were hung outside on a clothes line or throughout the house.

Samuel R. Scottron received his patent for the **curtain rod** in 1892. The rod was a long straight, metal tube with an opening at each end. The curtain rod made it possible for people to stop nailing curtains over windows.

One of the world's first **mops** was created by **Thomas Stewart** in 1893. The mop was made up of a long wooden handle with a cloth attached at the end, used to wash and dry floors. Before the mop, people cleaned floors on their hands and knees with a scrub brush.

Lloyd P. Ray improved the design of the **dust pan** in 1898, to pick up trash off the floor. The dust pan made it easier to dispose of trash. Before the dust pan, trash was swept out of the door or picked up with thin cardboard.

One of the world's first **street sweepers** was constructed by **Charles B. Brooks** in 1896. This invention was made up of large brushes attached to the bottom of a vehicle to clean away trash from the streets. Street sweepers are still used today in every major city in the United States to clean streets.

William B. Purvis invented an advanced version of the **fountain pen** in 1890. The fountain pen was hand-held with a supply of ink inside the pen. Purvis' invention was a major step forward. The fountain pen helped lead to the creation of the ballpoint pen which is currently used across the world by millions of people.

Jerome B. Rhodes invented an improved Water Closet in 1899. The **Water Closet** was the first indoor bathroom for homes. The water closet was an area the size of a closet that contained a toilet. Before the Water Closet was invented people had to go outside to a place called "the outhouse" to use the bathroom. Without J.B. Rhodes' invention and others like it, people everywhere would still have to go outside to the bathroom.

William B. Purvis built the first **paper bag machine** to cut and fold paper into bags in 1894. The paper bag machine changed the paper bag industry by speeding up production and reducing the cost of making bags.

Alexander Miles built an improved **elevator** in 1887, using automatic doors for the first time. Before Miles's invention, doors and openings to the elevator shaft were carelessly left open causing damage to packages and injury to passengers.

Ms. Lyda Newman developed one of the world's first plastic hair **brushes** in 1898. All types of brushes have been around for hundreds of years, but Ms. Newman invented one of the first modern plastic brush.

An improved **pencil sharpener** was created by **John L. Love** in 1897. Using a crank and rotor the pencil sharpener cut thin slices of the pencil away as the crank was turned to create a sharp point. Until the creation of the pencil sharpener, pencils had to be shaved with knives to produce a sharp point.

A team of African-Americans named **Albert Jones and Amos Long** received their patent on their invention that is widely used today, **caps for bottles** in 1898. They designed a round shaped metal covering for the purpose of sealing bottled liquids and jars. Bottles in the past used corks but the liquid often spoiled quickly. The caps for bottles allowed for liquids to be stored for a much longer period of time (up to several weeks). Caps for bottles changed the entire bottle-making industry.

Benjamin F. Jackson developed the **gas burner** in 1899 which is used in gas stoves and gas furnaces in homes and businesses around the world. The gas burner is a device that when lit, produces a flame for cooking or heating. Jackson's invention has made it possible to cook food and heat a house at the touch of a button. Before the gas burner, people had to gather wood from outside to create a fire, to cook food, and to heat the house.

John Albert Burr received a patent on the **lawn mower blades** he designed in 1899, his lawn mower consisted of rotary blades used to cut grass. Before this invention, the grass was cut by hand with a sickle, a curved single-edged blade on a short handle.

The **traffic light** was invented by **Garrett A. Morgan** in 1923. This invention not only shaped the way Americans drive but the entire world. Can you imagine the confusion between all the cars without the traffic light?

Packages Under 50 lbs Only

John Hunter built his **portable weighing scales** in 1896. The scales were made up of levers and balance springs to weigh letters and packages. Now there are portable weighing scales in post offices, hospitals, and businesses across the entire world.

Joseph W. Smith created his version of the lawn **sprinkler** in 1897, a swivel-shaped device that sprayed water over a large area. Before the lawn sprinkler, most lawns were watered by hand-held hoses.

The **water closet for railroad cars** was designed by **Lewis H. Latimer** in 1874. A compartment usually the size of a closet served as the toilet. This was the beginning of toilets being placed on trains, planes, and buses.

Lewis H. Latimer also designed the first **electric light bulb** with a carbon filament in 1881. Most history books credit Thomas Edison with this discovery, but his light bulb used a cotton filament. The cotton filament did not work very well, the light it produced lasted for a very short period of time. Latimer created the carbon filament light bulb that lasted much longer than the cotton filament. This invention brought America and the world out of the dark age of candles and into the age of the electric bulb. He went on to write the first book on lighting systems and supervised installation of the street lighting system in New York City, Philadelphia, Montreal, and London.

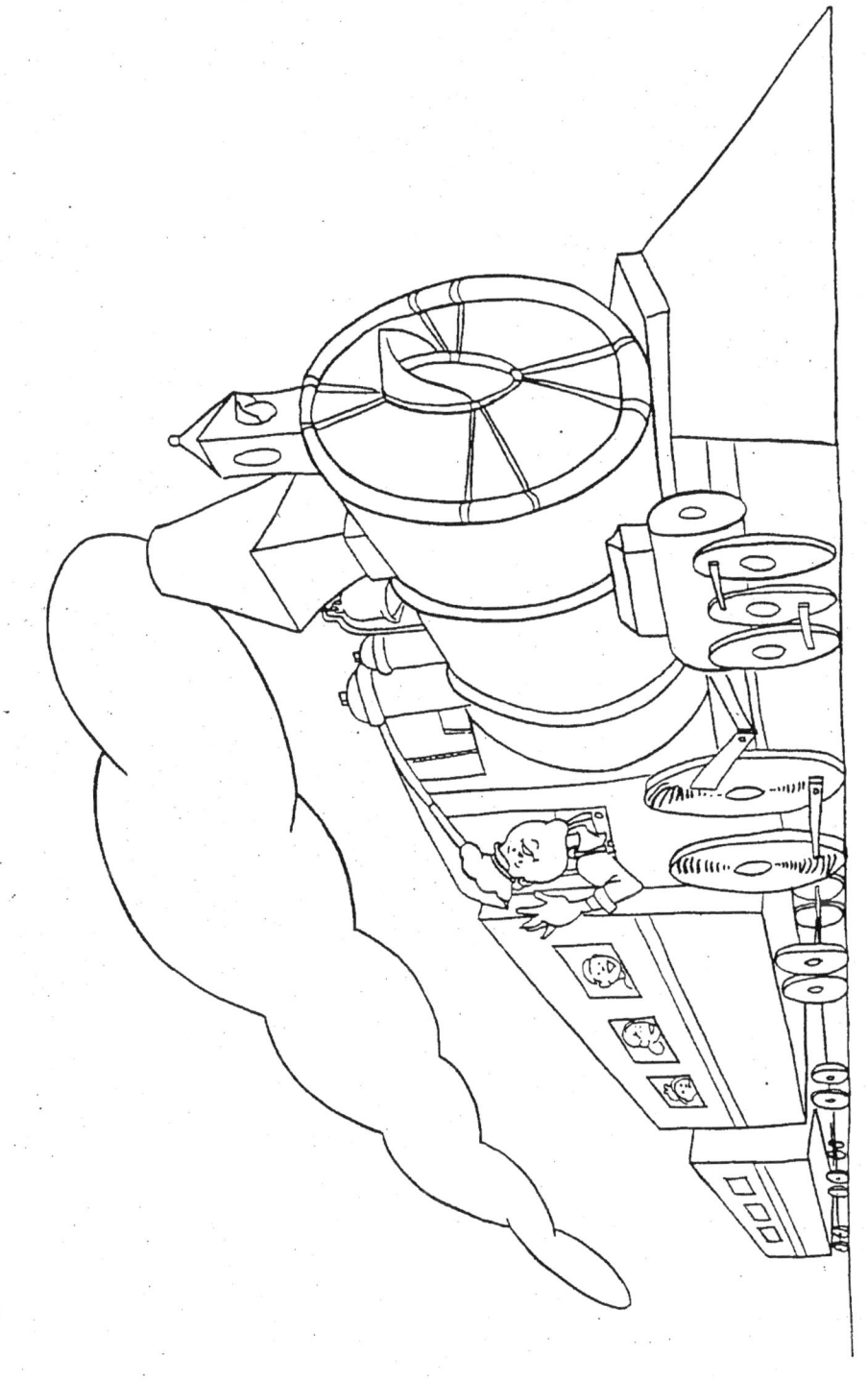

Landrow Bell received his patent for creating a better version of the **Locomotive Smoke Stack** in 1871. The cone-shaped metal structure was used to keep embers and cinders from blowing into passenger compartment. Before Bell's smoke stack, blowing embers and cinders from older smoke stacks often caused fires and injured passengers.

Garrett A. Morgan created the **gas mask** in 1914. This invention has made it possible for firemen and other rescue officers to enter smoke and gas-filled areas without inhaling smoke or gas. The gas mask has saved millions and millions of lives.

These inventions created by African-Americans have changed history. With an idea and a belief in themselves, African-Americans achieved what nobody else had achieved before them. These African-Americans have shown what you can do with an idea and a belief in yourself. **If you believe it, you can achieve it!!!**

The Original Patents

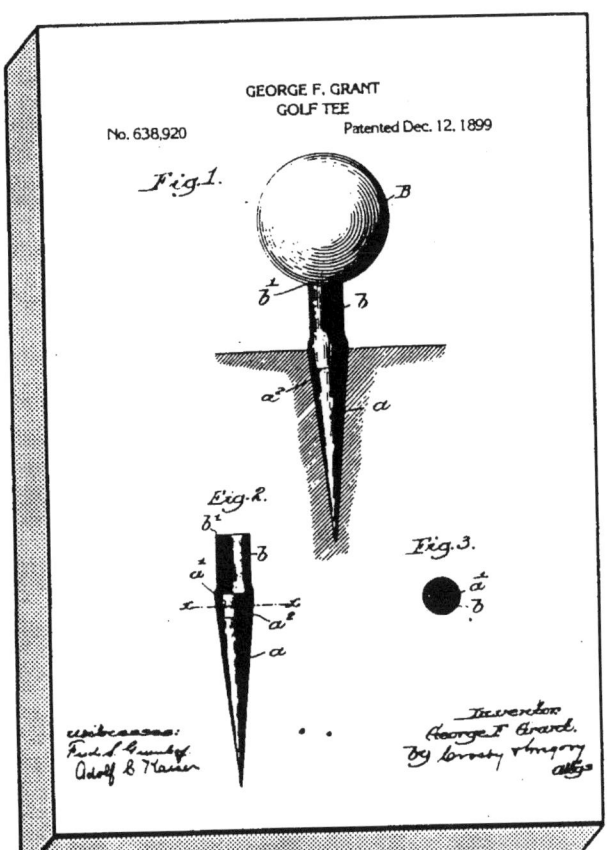

GEORGE F. GRANT
GOLF TEE

No. 638,920   Patented Dec. 12, 1899

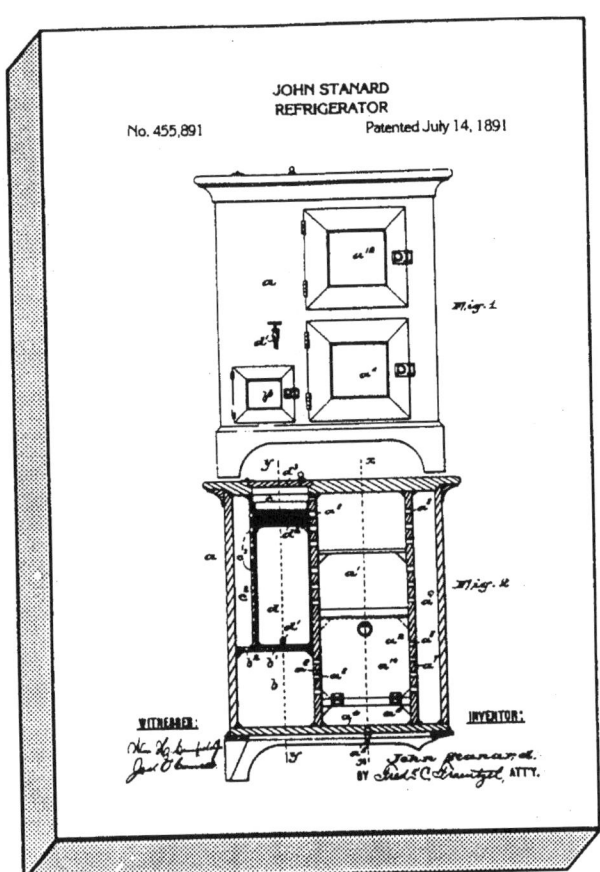

JOHN STANARD
REFRIGERATOR

No. 455,891   Patented July 14, 1891

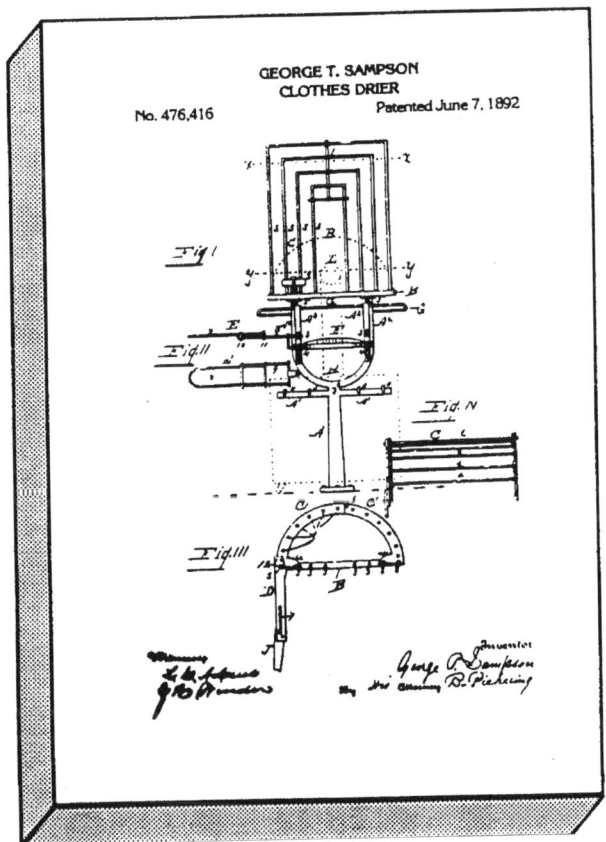

GEORGE T. SAMPSON
CLOTHES DRIER

No. 476,416   Patented June 7, 1892

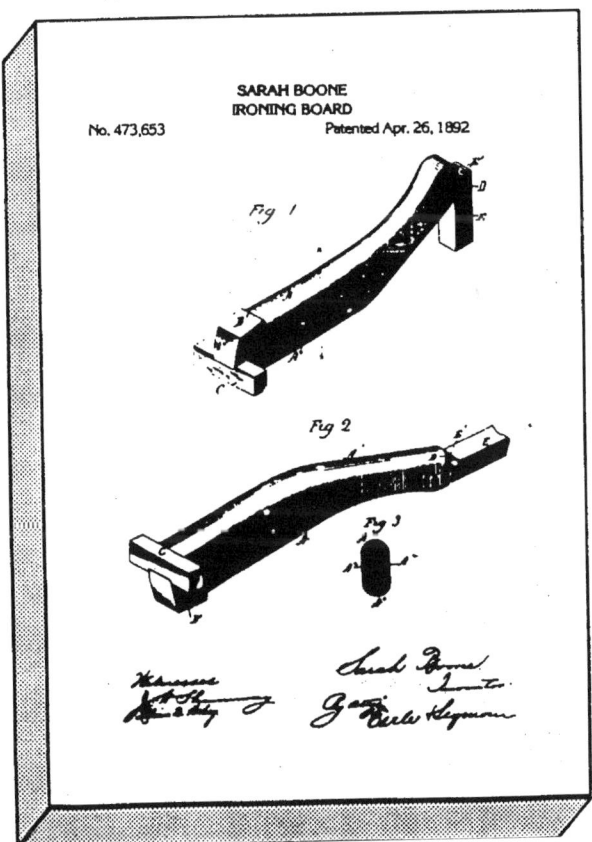

SARAH BOONE
IRONING BOARD

No. 473,653   Patented Apr. 26, 1892

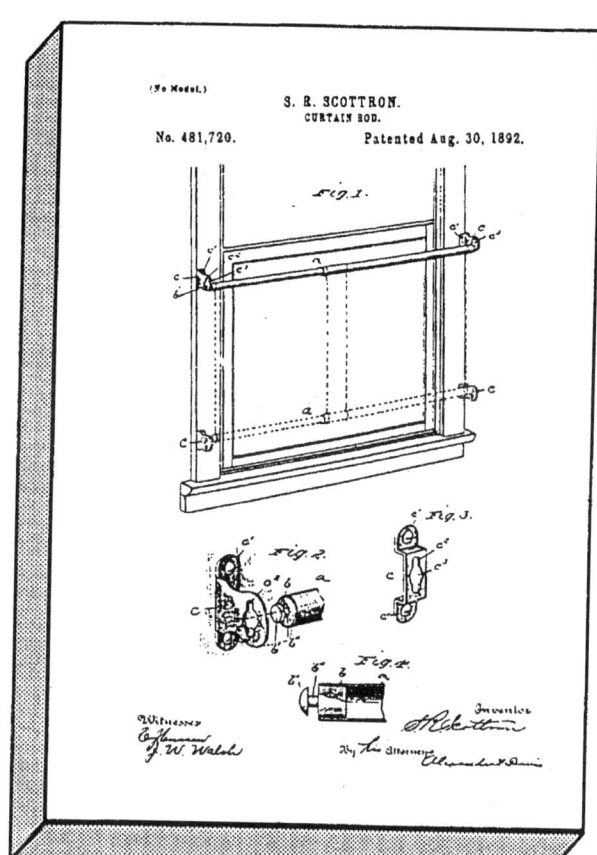

(No Model.)

S. R. SCOTTRON.
CURTAIN ROD.

No. 481,720.   Patented Aug. 30, 1892.

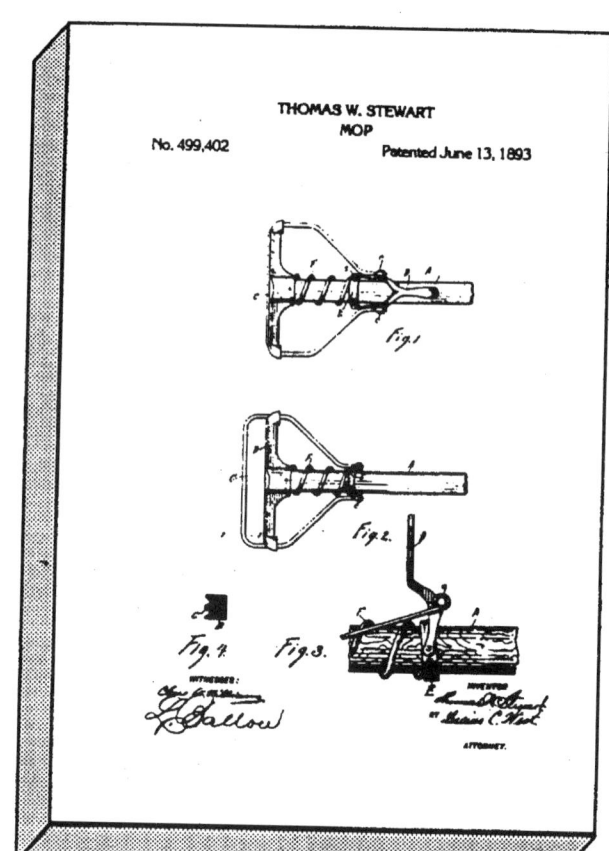

THOMAS W. STEWART
MOP

No. 499,402   Patented June 13, 1893

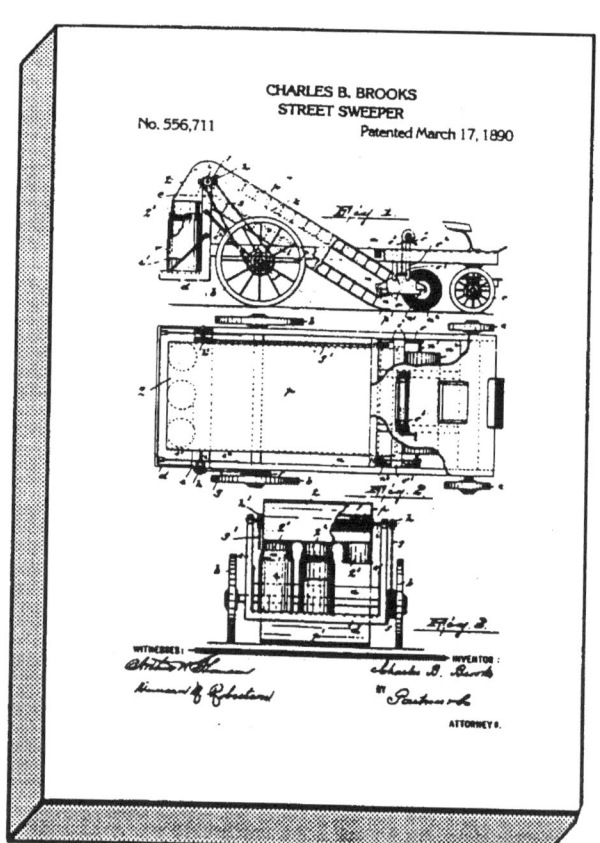

CHARLES B. BROOKS
STREET SWEEPER

No. 556,711   Patented March 17, 1890

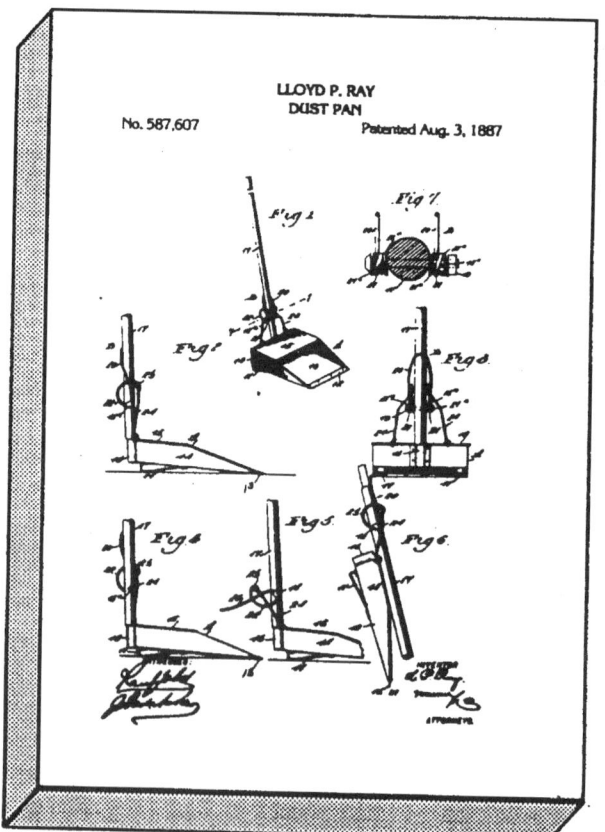

LLOYD P. RAY
DUST PAN

No. 587,607   Patented Aug. 3, 1887

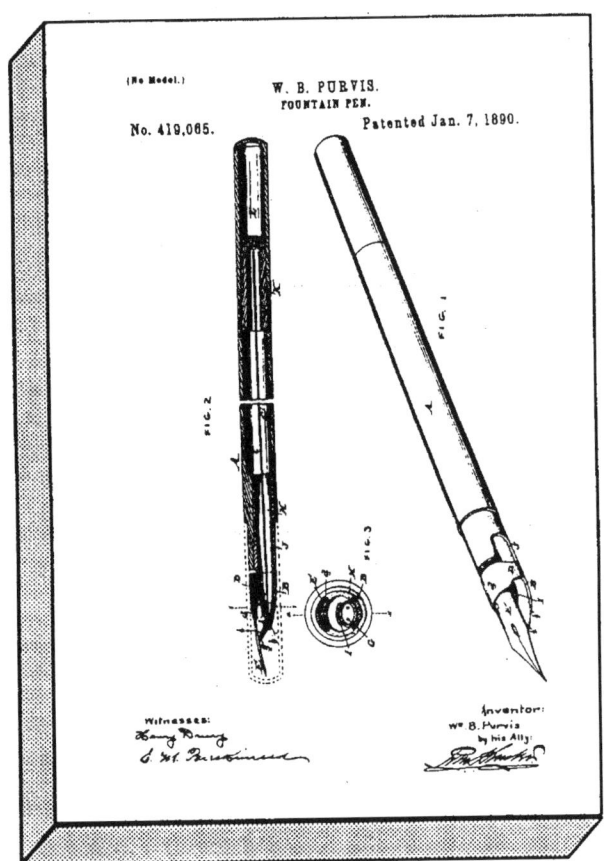

W. B. PURVIS.
FOUNTAIN PEN.

No. 419,065.   Patented Jan. 7, 1890.

FIG. 1
FIG. 2
FIG. 3

Witnesses:

Inventor:
Wm B. Purvis
by his Atty.

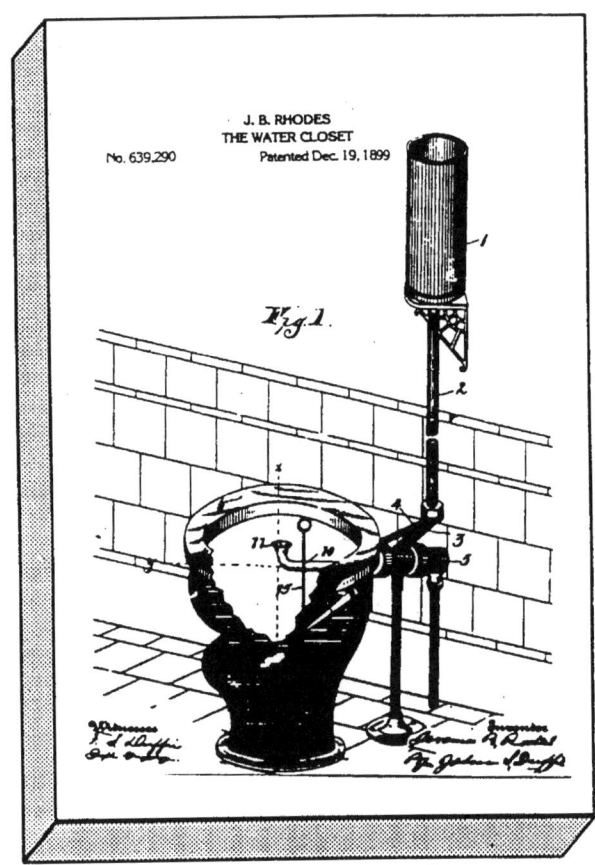

J. B. RHODES
THE WATER CLOSET

No. 639,290   Patented Dec. 19, 1899

Fig. 1

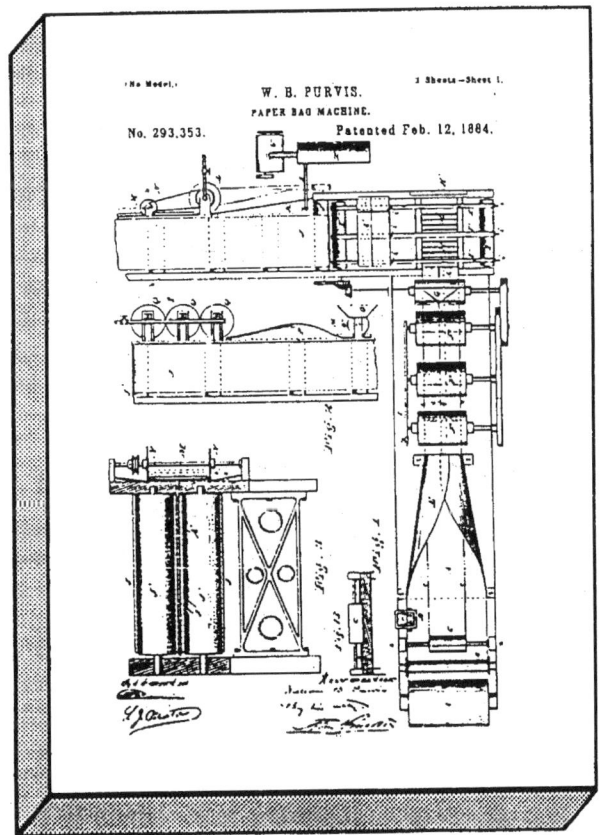

2 Sheets—Sheet 1.

W. B. PURVIS.
PAPER BAG MACHINE.

No. 293,353.   Patented Feb. 12, 1884.

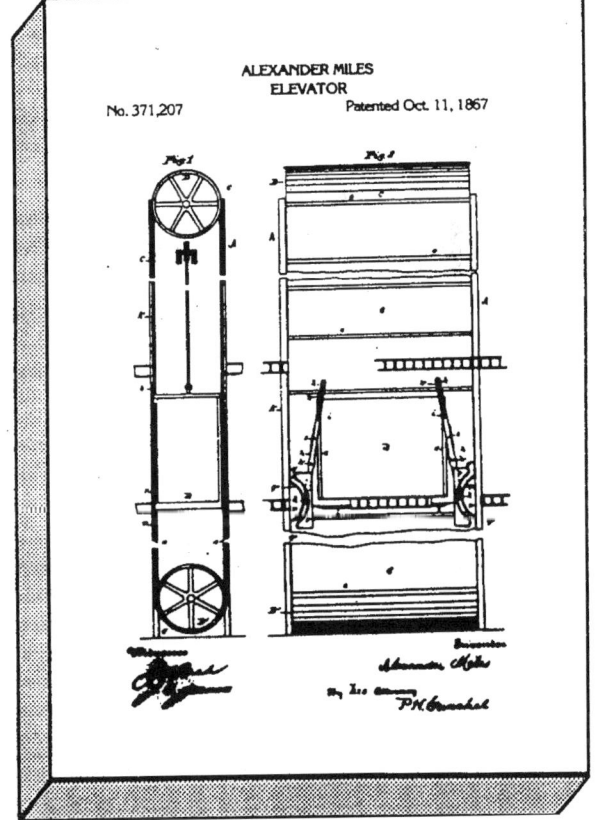

ALEXANDER MILES
ELEVATOR

No. 371,207   Patented Oct. 11, 1867

Fig. 1   Fig. 2

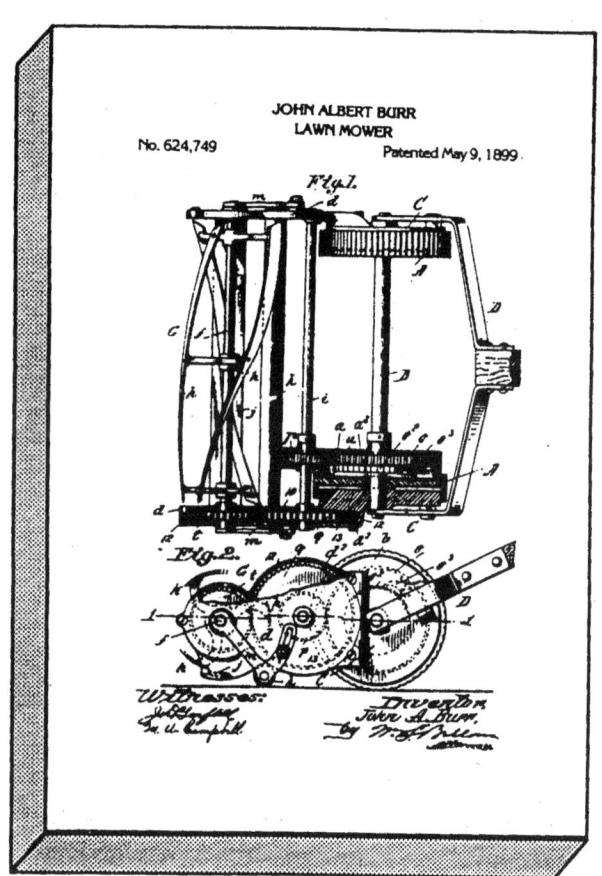

JOHN ALBERT BURR
LAWN MOWER

No. 624,749   Patented May 9, 1899.

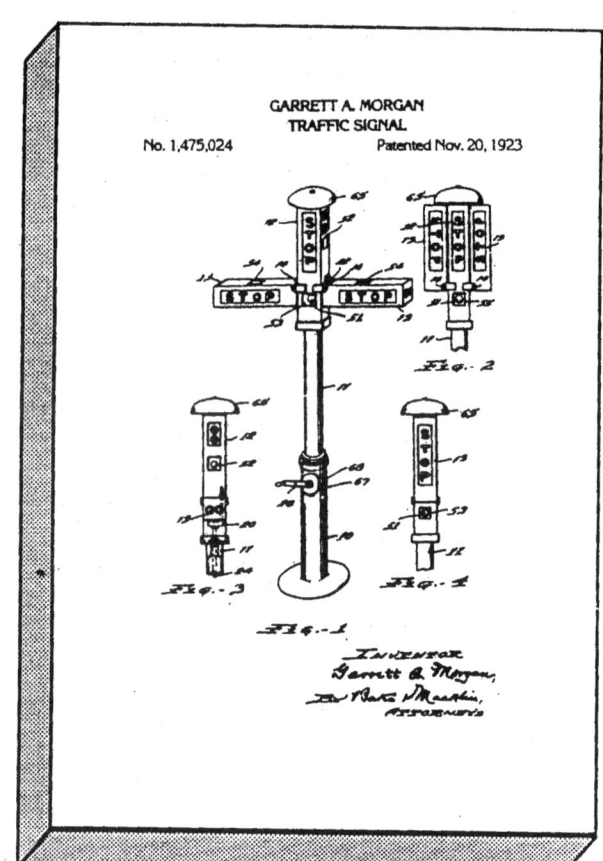

GARRETT A. MORGAN
TRAFFIC SIGNAL

No. 1,475,024   Patented Nov. 20, 1923

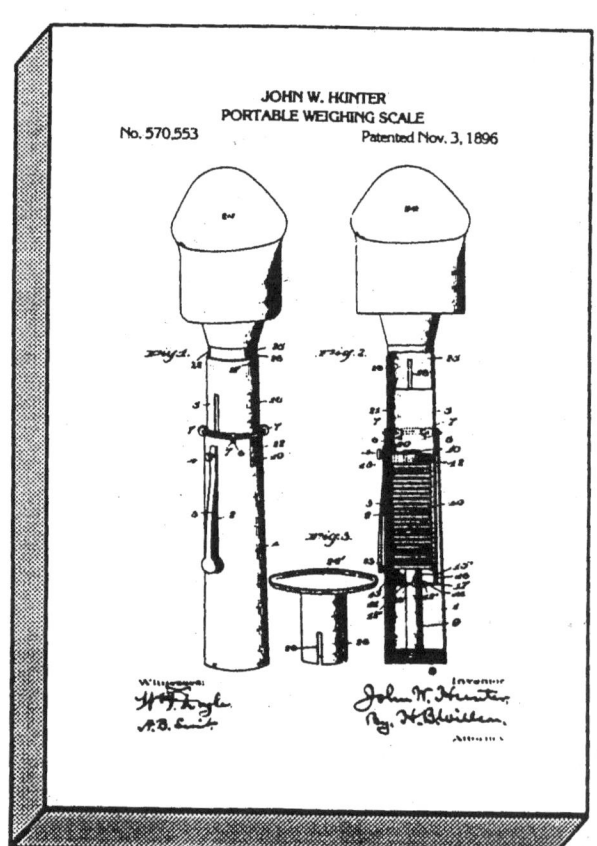

JOHN W. HUNTER
PORTABLE WEIGHING SCALE

No. 570,553   Patented Nov. 3, 1896

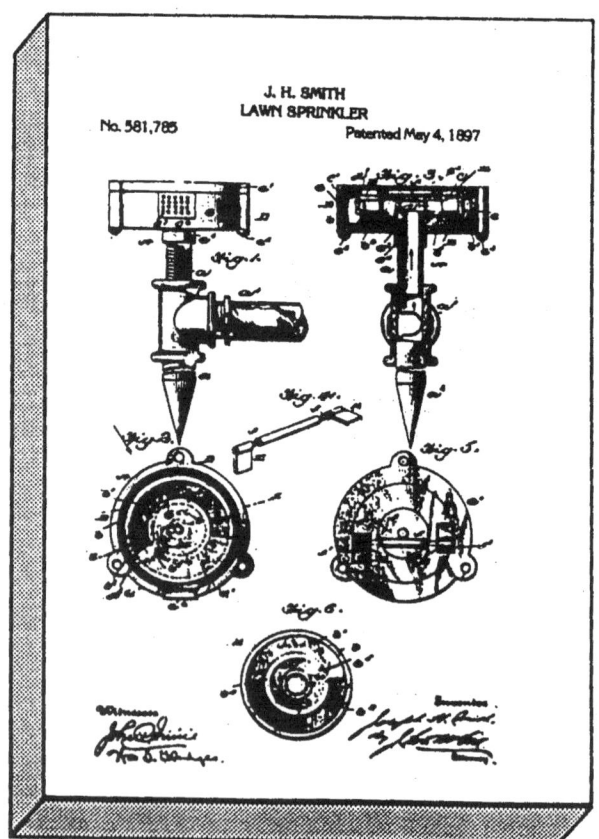

J. H. SMITH
LAWN SPRINKLER

No. 581,785   Patented May 4, 1897

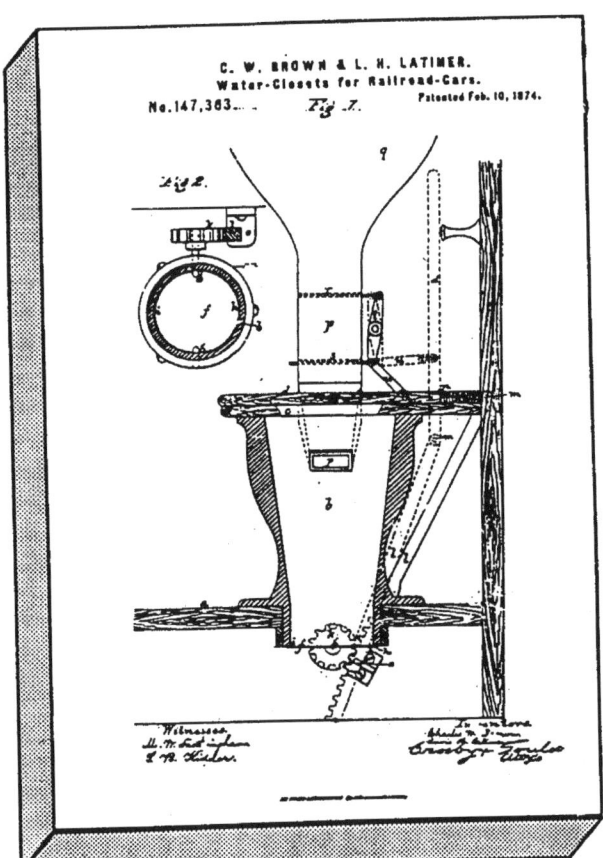

C. W. BROWN & L. H. LATIMER.
Water-Closets for Railroad-Cars.
No. 147,363. Fig. 1. Patented Feb. 10, 1874.

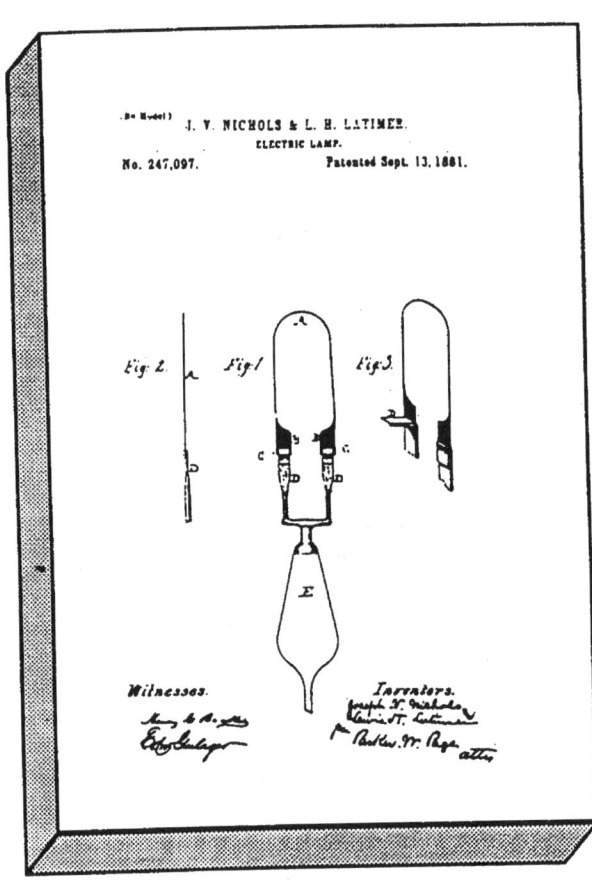

J. V. NICHOLS & L. H. LATIMER.
ELECTRIC LAMP.
No. 247,097. Patented Sept. 13, 1881.

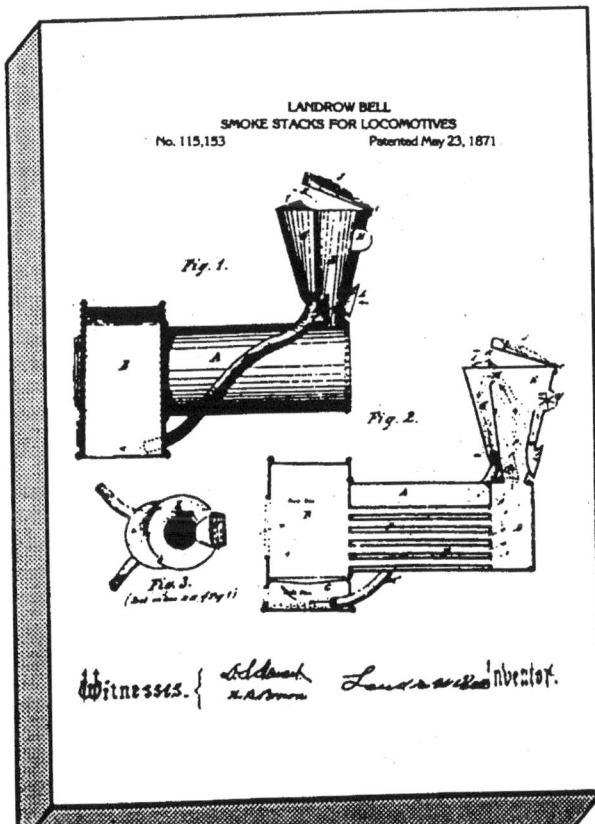

LANDROW BELL
SMOKE STACKS FOR LOCOMOTIVES
No. 115,153 Patented May 23, 1871

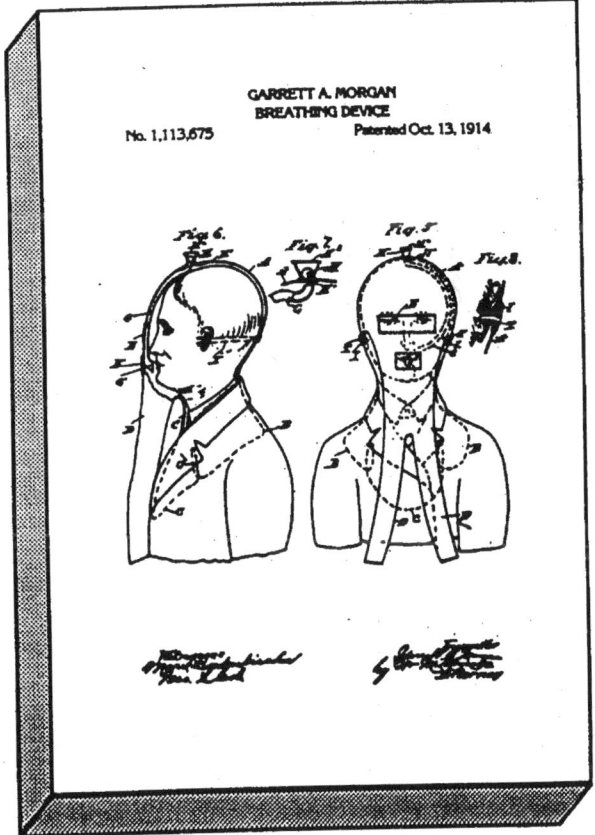

GARRETT A. MORGAN
BREATHING DEVICE
No. 1,113,675 Patented Oct. 13, 1914

Which two inventions were created by Garrett
Morgan? Draw and color each invention.

Draw and color the invention that helped clean
streets all over the country.

Draw and color two inventions that you can find in every school.

Draw and color every invention found in this book that a person would use to clean a house.

Draw and color the two inventions that have something to do with cutting and watering the grass.

Draw and color the invention that has helped people hang curtains all over the world.

Draw and color the two inventions created by W.B. Purvis.

Draw and color the invention created by George Grant.

Draw and color the inventions created by African American women.

Draw and color the invention created by Albert Jones and Amos Long.

JUStLiKe Me

A Coloring Book of Careers

Copyright © 1997 Just Like Me, Inc.

Text by
Yaba Baker

Illustrations by
Anne Marie Oldham

Just Like Me, Inc.
Washington, DC 20017
(202) 526-1725

Fifth Edition-Fifth Printing
September 2010

Do you ever think about what you will be when you grow up?

Will you be a doctor who helps people when they get sick?

You could be a scientist who makes medicine for the doctor to use on the patients.

Do you go to the movies? One day you could grow up to become a movie director.

Maybe if you like to swim, you could become a scuba diver.

If you like computers, you could become a computer programmer and design a new video game.

Will you own a business? You could own a toy company that makes toys for children across the world.

Do you like drawing? You could become an architect and design a house for your family.

You could be a pilot who flies all over the world.

If you like to cook, you could be a chef who cooks food
in a fancy restaurant.

Will you be a fireman who puts out fires in the neighborhood?

If you like music, you could become a musician and play the trumpet or sing in a concert in front of thousands of people.

Do you like to paint? You could become an artist and paint great works of art.

Will you be a policeman who helps to keep the neighborhood safe?

If you like to dance, you could become a dancer who performs on stage or on TV.

Will you be a photographer who takes pictures of families, sporting events, or weddings?

When you grow up you could be a lawyer who helps police put criminals away or help innocent people stay out of jail.

If you enjoy writing, you could become a reporter, editor, or if you work really hard, a publisher.

If you like to look at the stars, being an astronomer could be in your future. You could discover a new planet or a new solar system.

If you were an astronaut, you could be the first to walk on a new planet.

If you like boats, you could become a captain and sail all over the world.

If you become an engineer, you could design new cars, airplanes, or you could discover a new type of fuel to use instead of gas.

REPORT CARD	1	2	3	4	5	6
MATH	A	B	A	B	A	
ENGLISH	B	A	A⁺	A⁺	B	
SOCIAL STUDIES	A⁺	B	B⁺	A		
SCIENCE	A⁺	A	B⁺	A⁺		
FINE ARTS	B⁺	A⁺	A	B⁺		
COMPUTERS	A⁺	A⁺	A⁺	A⁺		

Graduation

Diploma!

Success!

You have so many careers to choose from, find what you like to do, then go for it!!
Whatever career you choose, you will have to work hard in school and get good
grades to achieve it. *If you believe it, and if you work at it, you will achieve it!!*

Draw and color the career or careers that you want to become when you grow-up.

Draw and color the career that sends you into space to explore different planets.

Draw and color the career that helps people build houses.

Draw two careers that involve taking pictures.

Draw a career that helps children learn their ABCs.

Draw a career that involves actors and actresses.

Draw two careers that involve medicine.

Draw two careers that involve sailing and swimming.

Draw two careers that help save lives.

Draw and color a career that cooks all types of foods.

Made in the USA
Lexington, KY
18 July 2014